W9-BGG-650

The European Union

Political, Social, and Economic Cooperation

THE
EUROPEAN UNION

POLITICAL, SOCIAL, AND ECONOMIC COOPERATION

SWEDEN

by
Heather Docalavich

Mason Crest Publishers
Philadelphia

Mason Crest Publishers Inc.
370 Reed Road, Broomall, Pennsylvania 19008
(866) MCP-BOOK (toll free)
www.masoncrest.com

J 914.85
Docalavich

First printing
1 2 3 4 5 6 7 8 9 10

Library of Congress Cataloging-in-Publication Data

Docalavich, Heather.
  Sweden / by Heather Docalavich.
      p. cm.—(The European Union)
  Includes index.
    ISBN 1-4222-0063-9
    ISBN 1-4222-0038-8 (series)
  1. Sweden—Juvenile literature. 2. European Union—Sweden—Juvenile literature. I. Title. II. European Union (Series) (Philadelphia, Pa.)
  DL609.D63 2006
  948.5—dc22
                              2005020927

Produced by Harding House Publishing Service, Inc.
www.hardinghousepages.com
Interior design by Benjamin Stewart.
Cover design by MK Bassett-Harvey.
Printed in the Hashemite Kingdom of Jordan.

CONTENTS

THE
EUROPEAN
UNION

GREENLAND SEA

BARENTS SEA

ICELAND
★ Reykjavik

NORWEGIAN SEA

WHITE SEA

RUSSIA

FINLAND
★ Tampere

NORWAY
Trondheim
Bergen · Lillehammer
Oslo

Turku · Helsinki

SWEDEN
Stockholm
Norrköping

Gulf of Bothnia
Bornäs

ESTONIA
Tartu
Tallin

Gulf of Finland

DENMARK
Kristiansand
Skagerrak
Aalborg
Odense · Malmö
Copenhagen
Helsingborg
Gothenburg

LATVIA
Ventspils · Riga
Liepāja · Daugavpils

Gulf of Riga

★ Moscow

UNITED KINGDOM
Glasgow · Edinburgh
Belfast

LITHUANIA
Klaipėda · Kaunas
Vilnius

RUSSIA

BELARUS
★ Minsk

IRELAND
Dublin
Killarney · Cork

NORTH SEA
Irish Sea
Liverpool · Manchester
Birmingham

BALTIC SEA

St. George's Channel

THE NETHERLANDS
Hamburg
Gdańsk

POLAND
Warsaw

The Hague · Amsterdam
Rotterdam
London
English Channel

Düsseldorf
Cologne

Berlin
Leipzig
Wrocław

BELGIUM
Brussels
LUXEMBOURG
Luxembourg
Paris

GERMANY
Frankfurt Main
Dresden

Kraków
Košice

UKRAINE
★ Kyiv

Nantes

Stuttgart
Prague
CZECH REPUBLIC
Brno

SLOVAKIA
Bratislava

MOLDOVA

Sea of Azov

FRANCE
Bordeaux
Bay of Biscay
Geneva · Lyons
SWITZERLAND
Bern

Munich
Salzburg
Linz
Vienna
AUSTRIA
Győr

Budapest
HUNGARY
Szeged

ROMANIA
★ Bucharest

BLACK SEA

Turin · Milan
Venice
Trieste
Ljubljana
SLOVENIA
Belgrade

Toulouse
Gulf du Lion
Marseille · Nice
Florence

CROATIA
BOSNIA-HERCEGOVINA
YUGOSLAVIA

BULGARIA
★ Sofia

PORTUGAL
Porto
Vigo
Bilbao

ITALY
Rome

ADRIATIC SEA

MACEDONIA

Thessaloniki

Lisbon
Madrid
Barcelona
Valencia

TYRRHENIAN SEA

ALBANIA

AEGEAN SEA

TURKEY
Ankara

SPAIN
Faro
Seville

Naples

IONIAN SEA

GREECE
Athens

Strait of Gibraltar

MEDITERRANEAN SEA

Kalamata
Sea of Crete

CYPRUS
Lefkosia (Nicosia)
Lemesos

SYRIA

LEBANON

MOROCCO
Rabat

ALGERIA

Tunis

MALTA
Valetta

MEDITERRANEAN SEA

JORDAN
Damascus

ISRAEL & THE PALESTINIAN TERRITORIES

TUNISIA

Tripoli

Cairo

LIBYA

EGYPT

SWEDEN

European Union Member since 1995

Kiruna

Gällivare

Boden

Piteå

Skellefteå

Umeå

Örnsköldsvik

Östersund

Härnösand

Sundsvall

Hudiksvall

Söderhamn

Gävle

Uppsala

Stockholm ☆

Norrköping

Linköping

Borås

Göteborg

Helsingborg

Malmö

INTRODUCTION

Sixty years ago, Europe lay scarred from the battles of the Second World War. During the next several years, a plan began to take shape that would unite the countries of the European continent so that future wars would be inconceivable. On May 9, 1950, French Foreign Minister Robert Schuman issued a declaration calling on France, Germany, and other European countries to pool together their coal and steel production as "the first concrete foundation of a European federation." "Europe Day" is celebrated each year on May 9 to commemorate the beginning of the European Union (EU).

The EU consists of twenty-five countries, spanning the continent from Ireland in the west to the border of Russia in the east. Eight of the ten most recently admitted EU member states are former communist regimes that were behind the Iron Curtain for most of the latter half of the twentieth century.

Any European country with a democratic government, a functioning market economy, respect for fundamental rights, and a government capable of implementing EU laws and policies may apply for membership. Bulgaria and Romania are set to join the EU in 2007. Croatia and Turkey have also embarked on the road to EU membership.

While the EU began as an idea to ensure peace in Europe through interconnected economies, it has evolved into so much more today:

- Citizens can travel freely throughout most of the EU without carrying a passport and without stopping for border checks.

- EU citizens can live, work, study, and retire in another EU country if they wish.

- The euro, the single currency accepted throughout twelve of the EU countries (with more to come), is one of the EU's most tangible achievements, facilitating commerce and making possible a single financial market that benefits both individuals and businesses.

- The EU ensures cooperation in the fight against cross-border crime and terrorism.

- The EU is spearheading world efforts to preserve the environment.

- As the world's largest trading bloc, the EU uses its influence to promote fair rules for world trade, ensuring that globalization also benefits the poorest countries.

- The EU is already the world's largest donor of humanitarian aid and development assistance, providing 55 percent of global official development assistance to developing countries in 2004.

The EU is neither a nation intended to replace existing nations, nor an international organization. The EU is unique—its member countries have established common institutions to which they delegate some of their sovereignty so that decisions on matters of joint interest can be made democratically at the European level.

Europe is a continent with many different traditions and languages, but with shared values such as democracy, freedom, and social justice, cherished values well known to North Americans. Indeed, the EU motto is "United in Diversity."

Enjoy your reading. Take advantage of this chance to learn more about Europe and the EU!

Ambassador John Bruton,
Head of Delegation of the European Commission, Washington, D.C.

Kalmar castle on one of Sweden's lakes

CHAPTER 1   THE LANDSCAPE

Sweden occupies the eastern portion of northern Europe's Scandinavian Peninsula. Slightly larger than the state of California and nearly the same shape, Sweden is the largest and most populous nation in Scandinavia. The Swedes call their country, *Sverige*, which means "the land of the Sveas," after the ancient inhabitants of the region. Stockholm is the country's capital

One of the world's northernmost nations, Sweden extends nearly 1,000 miles (1,600 kilometers) from north to south, and one-seventh of its territory lies above the Arctic Circle. Thick glaciers of the last ice age shaped the land, rounding mountaintops, carving out deep valleys, and digging long **fjords** into the coastline. Almost 100,000 lakes created by this glacial activity dot the countryside and cover about one-twelfth of the nation's total area.

Sweden shares a hilly border with Norway to the west, and a narrow border with Finland to the northeast. The remainder of the nation borders the sea. The Gulf of Bothnia and the Baltic Sea lie to the east. Waterways separate Sweden from Denmark: the Skagerrak, Kattegat, and Öresund straits lie to the south and southwest. Two large islands in the Baltic Sea, Gotland and Öland, are also Swedish territories. Thousands of tiny rock-covered islands are scattered along Sweden's Baltic coastline, protecting the mainland from the open sea.

HIGHLANDS, MARSH, AND WOODLANDS

Sweden can be separated into three distinct regions: *Norrland*, or Northland, in the north; *Svealand*, or Land of the Swedes, in the center; and *Götaland*, or Land of the Goths, in the south.

Norrland accounts for almost 70 percent of Sweden's land area but is home to only about 15 percent of the population. Far to the north, inside the Arctic Circle, is Saamiland, a region inhabited by the Saami people. The land is largely treeless and barren, with extensive stretches of highlands that hold rich mineral deposits. Sweden's highest peak, Kebnekaise, rises to 6,926 feet (2,111 meters) in Saamiland. The central area of Norrland is relatively flat and marked by marshlands, peat bogs, and dense stands of forest—mostly Scotch pine and Norwegian spruce. Long narrow lakes, rough stretches of river, and rocky glacial hills known as moraines interrupt the landscape. Farther to the south, the land is more developed and features agricultural and industrial regions with richer soils and Sweden's most important iron ore deposits.

Svealand is also heavily wooded, although more of this region has been cleared for farming and urban development, particularly around the cities of Stockholm and Uppsala. The land in central Svealand is generally low and flat with rich soil. Many of Sweden's largest lakes are located in Svealand.

In Götaland, south of the central lowlands, the land begins to rise and form the highlands of Småland. This area is similar to the moraine and peat bog region of Norrland, except that it has a warmer climate. At the southern edge of Sweden,

Farm in Smaland

the land drops again to form the low agricultural plain of the province of Skåne. This highly developed agricultural region is densely populated and is known as Sweden's breadbasket.

Southeast of Stockholm in the Baltic Sea are Sweden's two largest islands, Öland and Gotland. Öland, covering 519 square miles (1,344 square kilometers), and Gotland, covering 1,210 square miles (3,140 square kilometers), are generally flat. The islands have a **maritime** climate and are home to a great variety of unusual plants. Sandy beaches can be found in many places, making the islands popular vacation destinations. Many smaller islands can also be found in the waters off the Swedish coast.

Gothenberg Lighthouse off Sweden's coast

RIVERS AND LAKES

Sweden has about 100,000 lakes and many rapid, turbulent rivers. Most major rivers are in Norrland and flow in a south-easterly direction toward the Gulf of Bothnia and the Baltic Sea. The rivers, which are often connected to long, narrow lakes, are a valuable source of hydroelectric power. They are also used as an important source of transport for logs in Sweden's thriving lumber industry. Sweden's principal rivers are the Ångermanälven, Dalälven, Trysilelva, Ume Alven, and Torneälven.

In the south-central area of the country, known as the lake district, are two lakes: the Vänern, which covers 2,156 square miles (5,584 square kilometers), is Europe's third-largest lake; the Vättern, which covers 740 square miles (1,910 square kilometers), is Sweden's second-largest lake, after Vänern. The two lakes, together with several smaller lakes, rivers, and canals, form an important domestic water route called the Göta Canal. Originally built in the early nineteenth century, the Göta Canal extends for about 240 miles (about 386 kilometers) and provides a critical transportation link between the Baltic Sea, Stockholm, and other cities. Other important lakes in the district include Mälaren, Hjälmaren, and Siljan.

QUICK FACTS: THE GEOGRAPHY OF SWEDEN

Location: Northern Europe, bordering the Baltic Sea, Gulf of Bothnia, Kattegat, and Skagerrak, between Finland and Norway
Area: slightly larger than California
  total: 173,732 square miles (449,964 sq. km.)
  land: 158,663 square miles (410,934 sq. km.)
  water: 15,070 square miles (39,030 sq. km.)
Borders: Finland 382 miles (614 km.), Norway 1,006 miles (1,619 km.)
Climate: temperate in south with cold, cloudy winters and cool, partly cloudy summers; subarctic in north
Terrain: mostly flat or gently rolling lowlands; mountains in the west
Elevation extremes:
  lowest point: reclaimed bay of Lake Hammarsjon (near Kristianstad)— –8 feet (–2.41 meters)
  highest point: Kebnekaise—6,926 feet (2,111 meters)
Natural hazards: ice floes, especially in the Gulf of Bothnia, can interfere with marine traffic

Source: www.cia.gov, 2005.

A VARIED CLIMATE

Although a significant portion of Sweden's land lies north of the Arctic Circle, the Swedish climate is much milder than that of most other countries located equally as far north. Sweden's relatively moderate climate results from the warming influence of winds blowing across the Gulf Stream, which sweep over Sweden from the North Atlantic Ocean. In winter, these warming influences are offset by cold air masses that come in from the north and east.

Northern Sweden's climate is much more severe than that of the south, primarily because elevations are higher and the mountains block the warming marine winds. The average temperature in February, the coldest month, is below freezing throughout Sweden, with an average temperature range in Stockholm of 22° to 30°F (–5° to –1°C), in Göteborg of 25° to 34°F (–4° to 1°C), and in Piteå, in the northern part of the country, of 6° to 22°F (–14° to –6°C). In July, the warmest month, the average temperature range is 56° to 71°F (13° to 22°C) in Stockholm, 56° to 69°F (13° to 21°C) in Göteborg, and 53° to 69°F (12° to 21°C) in Piteå. North of the Arctic Circle, daylight is continuous for about two months in summer, while continuous darkness occurs for about two months in winter. Ice covers all lakes for more than a hundred days a year in the south and more than two hundred days a year in the far north. The Gulf of Bothnia typically begins to freeze over near the shore in late November, and the ice usually lasts until the approach of summer in June. Fog is common all along the Swedish coastline.

Precipitation is relatively low across the country except in the higher mountain regions. Rainfall is heaviest in the mountains along the Norwegian border and in the southwest. Most rain falls in the late summer. During the winter months, heavy snows are common in central and northern Sweden.

TREES, PLANTS, AND WILDLIFE

Arctic vegetation prevails in northern Sweden. The highest mountain areas are barren of all vegetation. The next highest regions are the moorlands, which are inhabited by various kinds of mosses, lichens, and a few species of hardy flowering plants. South of the moorlands is an area of birch and willow trees, although because of the harsh conditions, these trees are often dwarfed and stunted. The next lower, and largest, region is covered with **coniferous** forest. This immense forest belt stretches across more than six hundred miles (950 kilometers) with a width that ranges from 100 miles to more than 150 miles (160 kilometers to more than 240 kilometers). In the south, **deciduous** trees, such as oak, beech, elm, and maple, can be found. On the islands of Gotland and Öland, the mild climate encourages the growth of walnut, acacia, and mulberry trees.

Roe deer and moose are common in Swedish forests. Reindeer are common in the north, where they are herded by the Saami. Bears, lynx, and wolves, although once plentiful, are now quite rare. Lemmings are plentiful in the northern moorlands. Various wild birds are abundant, with many rare species protected in nature preserves.

Fish thrive in the North and Baltic seas and in Sweden's lakes and rivers. Principal marine varieties include mackerel, herring, and cod; freshwater varieties include pike, perch, whiting, and trout. Salmon are found in both fresh- and saltwater. Shellfish, including lobsters and prawns, are found in coastal waters. Thousands of seals live in the waters around Sweden. In 1988, an outbreak of a deadly disease called phocine distemper virus (PDV) wiped out as much as 65 percent of the seal population in the North and Baltic seas. Thankfully, in recent years the seal population has largely bounced back. Sweden has adopted EU standards for environmental protection and operates several national parks and protected nature areas.

Sweden's patchwork landscape

Kalmar castle is a reminder of Sweden's history

2 SWEDEN'S HISTORY AND GOVERNMENT

Sweden is an ancient nation that has existed as an independent and sovereign country for hundreds of years. Signs of human habitation can be found in Sweden dating back more than 11,000 years. Ancient petroglyphs, images carved by prehistoric peoples on natural rock surfaces, from that era can be found all across Sweden. These images are thought to be the earliest form of non-written communication. The earliest images can be found in the northern province of Jämtland, and depict the hunting of wild animals such as elk, reindeer, bears, and seals.

SWEDEN IN THE IRON AGE

In the year 98, the Roman historian Tacitus described a tribe of people called the Suiones living on an island in the sea. These Suiones had ships that were noteworthy because of their distinctive shape with a prow on both ends. Today we recognize that shape as the classic Viking ship. The name *Suiones* refers to the peoples the Anglo-Saxons knew as *Sweons*, whose country was called Sweoland. In the epic *Beowulf*, this tribe is also called Sweoeod.

By the sixth century, the Ostrogoth historian Jordanes also wrote about the Suiones. Several

Seventeenth-century map of Sweden

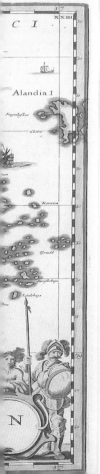

independent historical sources mention a number of Swedish kings who lived during this period. At that time, kings were warlords rather than kings as we understand that title today, and their lands were a number of petty kingdoms whose borders changed constantly as the kings battled and killed each other. The politics of these early kingdoms are retold in *Beowulf* and the Norse sagas.

The period between 793 and 1066 is known as the Viking Age; this corresponds to the latter half of the Iron Age. During this period, the Vikings—warriors and traders from Sweden, Denmark, and Norway—raided and explored large parts of Europe, the Middle East, northern Africa, and even the coast of North America.

The longships used by the Vikings were the most technologically sophisticated of their day. Uniquely suited to both deep and shallow waters, these ships extended the reach of Norse raiders, traders, and settlers not only along coastlines, but also along the major rivers of Europe. The Viking leader Rurik founded the first Russian state with a capital at Novgorod. Other explorers from modern-day Sweden continued south on rivers to the Black Sea and went on to establish trade with Constantinople.

Swedish Vikings also played a role in Western Europe later in the Viking period. During the conquest of England under the Danish king Svein Forkbeard, Swedes, along with Norwegians, were recruited as **mercenaries** to aid in the invasion. Monuments in Sweden attest to the skills of warriors who returned home rich in plunder from English campaigns. Swedes were later recruited by the infamous Norwegian king Harald to help him regain control of Norway. These Swedish mercenaries subsequently helped Harald invade England in 1066, where he and his army were destroyed, marking the end of the Viking Age.

CHRISTIANIZATION AND THE EARLY SWEDISH KINGS

About the beginning of the tenth century, historical records note a king named Erik, whose kingdom seems to have reached as far as Norway. Later, another king named Björn is said to have been the son of Erik and to have reigned for fifty years. Björn's successors were his sons Olof and Eric, also known as Eric the Victorious. Following Olof's death, his son Styrbjörn was refused his share of power by Eric. Eventually, Styrbjörn attacked Eric, and a battle was fought between the two, during which Styrbjörn was defeated and killed. Eric himself died ten years after this battle, around 993. According to the story, he had obtained victory from the god Odin in return for a promise to give himself to the gods at the end of ten years.

Eric's son Olof succeeded him as king and instituted Christianity as the state religion. For the next 280 years, the land was ruled by a series of kings who gained and lost territory through long years of almost unending warfare. During this period, the newly Christian Swedes broke with the Roman Catholic Church and established the Church of Sweden. By 1275, the Swedish king, Magnus Ladulås found himself the leader of a heavily divided nation. Lesser rulers waged constant battles over small tracts of land, and the security of Swedish territory was threatened by enemies abroad who sought to take advantage of the country's instability.

King Magnus introduced a **feudal** system similar to that already established elsewhere in Europe, and as a result, the warring factions of Sweden were once more reunited. Magnus also promoted the formation of separate classes by extending the privileges of the clergy and instituting the **landed nobility**. Knights (lesser nobles and men of the upper middle class) now formed a heavily armed cavalry as the core of the national army. The period of Magnus's reign marks the rise of a prominent merchant class, as the towns now began to acquire charters. By the beginning of the fourteenth century, **codified** laws appeared, and the king and his council began to perform legislative functions.

Unfortunately, after the king's death, some of the instability returned as different nobles fought for the throne. The Swedes were briefly united with Norway in 1319, but various power struggles continued as a succession of kings were overthrown by their nephews and cousins. Eventually, at the request of the Swedish nobility, the Swedes formed an alliance with Queen Margaret of Denmark, becoming subjects of the Danish throne in what became known as the Kalmar Union.

THE KALMAR UNION

The Kalmar Union was formed by Queen Margaret I of Denmark in the Swedish town of Kalmar, then close to the Danish border. The Swedish king Albert, born in Germany, was disliked by the Swedish nobility, and their rebellion had received help from the Danes, who intended the union to serve as protection from the growing power of the Germans. As a result, Margaret united the three kingdoms of Denmark, Norway, and Sweden under a single monarch.

Eventually, the Swedes became unhappy with the Danes' frequent wars, which disturbed Swedish commerce. Also, the centralization of government in Denmark caused resentment. The Swedish nobility wanted to retain a substantial degree of self-government. The union began to dissolve in 1430, and ultimately, an armed rebellion led to the expulsion of Danish forces from Sweden. When the reigning king died childless in 1448, Sweden elected Charles VIII as their king, with the intent of reestablishing the union under a Swedish crown. Charles was elected king of Norway in the following year, but the counts of Holstein were more influential than the Swedes and the Norwegians together, and they made the Danes appoint Christian I of Oldenburg as king. The ensuing struggle for power

Sweden's stone fences mark ancient boundary lines.

The Royal Mounted Guard carry the pride of Sweden's history.

between Sweden and Denmark dominated the union for another seventy years.

The harsh policies of the Danes eventually led to the end of their rule over Sweden. After the bloody retaking of Sweden by Christian II in 1520 and the subsequent massacre of Swedish patriots, known as the Stockholm bloodbath, the Swedes started yet another revolt, which ousted the Danish forces once and for all in 1521. Independence was regained with the election of

King Gustav of the Vasa on June 6, 1523, restoring sovereignty for Sweden and finally dissolving the Kalmar Union.

THE RISE OF SWEDISH POWER

Gustav fought for an independent Sweden, crushing attempts to restore the Kalmar Union and laying the foundations of modern Sweden. At the same time, he broke with the Catholic Church. In 1517, Martin Luther, a German monk, led a revolt against the Roman Catholic Church. Lutheranism, the religious philosophy established by Luther, quickly gained a following across Europe. When the Roman Catholic Church supported the Danish king as the rightful ruler of Sweden, Gustav declared a split with Rome and appointed his own bishops to institute Lutheran reforms in the Church of Sweden. He also seized all Church holdings, thus stripping Rome of its wealth and influence in Sweden.

During the seventeenth century, Sweden emerged victorious in wars against Denmark-Norway, Russia, and Poland. Sweden, with about one million inhabitants, was beginning to emerge as a major European power. Following the Peace of Westphalia in 1648, Sweden ruled the Russian province of Ingria (in which Saint Petersburg later would be founded), Estonia, Livonia, and even some major coastal towns and other areas of northern Germany. By 1658, Sweden had also acquired important provinces in Denmark and Norway.

The increasing wealth and power of the Swedes did not go unnoticed by their neighbors. Russia, Poland, and Denmark-Norway formed a military alliance in 1700 and attacked the Swedish empire. Although the young Swedish king Charles XII won some important victories in the early years of the Great Northern War, his decision to attack Russia proved disastrous. With Swedish forces spread too thinly to adequately defend all fronts, the Swedes began to experience a series of defeats.

King Charles was killed during a battle in Norway in 1718. At the war's end, the allied powers, joined by Prussia and England, ended Sweden's brief period of glory by seizing her foreign holdings and introducing a fifty-year period of limited monarchy under parliamentary rule. In 1772, a bloodless ***coup d'état*** led by King Gustav III resulted in the return of ***absolute monarchy***, a state of affairs that would last until limited monarchy returned following Sweden's involvement in the Napoleonic Wars of the nineteenth century.

MODERNIZATION OF SWEDEN

The late nineteenth century was an important period of modernization and industrialization for Sweden. The nation's predominantly agricultural economy began to shift to a more industrialized economy. Unfortunately, wealth and prosperity did not increase at the same rate as the population. About one million Swedes immigrated to the United States between 1850 and 1890.

Many important developments occurred during this period, including the foundation of a modern free press, the abolition of **trade monopolies** in manufacturing to better promote free enterprise, the reform of national taxation and voting laws, the introduction of national military service, and the beginning of a multiparty political system. By the end of the century, three major political parties operated in Sweden: the Social Democrat Party, the Liberal Party, and the Conservative Party.

As the twentieth century dawned, the nation saw even greater changes. Industry continued to grow in importance to the national economy. **Suffrage** was expanded to include all men over the age of twenty-one, and sweeping labor reforms were made to improve working conditions in factories and limit the long hours worked by children. Sweden was once again growing in prosperity and influence when World War I swept across Europe.

World War I began on June 28, 1914, when Gavrilo Princip, a Serbian **nationalist**, assassinated Austrian archduke Franz Ferdinand and his wife, Sophie. Russia allied with Serbia. Germany sided with Austria and soon declared war on Russia. After France declared its support for Russia, Germany attacked France. German troops then invaded Belgium, a **neutral** country, as it stood between German forces and Paris. Great Britain eventually declared war on Germany. Soon the United States and other nations around the world were at war. Partially because of Sweden's out-of-the-way location, and partly because of the high demand on both sides for Swedish steel, ball bearings, wood pulp, and matches, Sweden was able not only to remain neutral throughout the conflict but also to profit from it.

The wealth Sweden accumulated during the war helped to buffer the effects of the worldwide depression that struck in the 1930s. During this period, the Swedes instituted many welfare policies regarding financial assistance for the unemployed, the disabled, and the elderly, which are the foundations of **welfare state** seen in Sweden tod

Another result of World War I wa: nition by Sweden that declaring neutr a time of war was not necessarily a g escaping the conflict. Having seen t

The royal crown and orbs

and occupation of other neutral territories during the war, Sweden began to invest in its military, determined to have the equipment and manpower to defend itself in case of foreign invasion. This proved to be very insightful planning.

WORLD WAR II AND SWEDEN TODAY

As Sweden increased its social welfare structure and military capabilities, the hardships faced in other parts of Europe that were devastated by the

Great Depression caused great unrest. In Germany, the Nazi Party grew powerful, attracting members by offering radical solutions to the country's economic problems and upholding patriotic values. The Nazis' leader, Adolf Hitler, had ambitious plans for Germany's future.

Soon after being appointed **chancellor** in 1933, Adolf Hitler became a dictator. Hitler wanted to rebuild the German military power it had lost in World War I. In 1936, he formed an

By the time World War II ended, Sweden had increased its airpower tenfold.

alliance with Italy and signed an anticommunist agreement with Japan. These three powers became known as the Axis powers. France, Great Britain, and the countries that were allied with them became known simply as the Allies.

Hitler's stated goal of reclaiming German lands lost in World War I was initially accepted by the Allies, and a policy known as appeasement was developed that granted a series of concessions to Hitler in hopes of preventing another war. This ultimately proved unsuccessful, and Hitler's armies swept across Europe as World War II began.

Sweden once again proclaimed its neutrality in the conflict. However, Swedish policy during World War II had some distinct differences from the policies pursued during World War I. This time, the Swedes engaged in a policy known as armed neutrality. This meant that the draft was in effect, and all able-bodied soldiers were called to join the armed forces in case of foreign invasion. To pacify Nazi aggression, the Swedes allowed German troops to make use of a few railroads for transporting men and supplies, and Sweden continued to trade with both sides throughout the war.

The Swedish policy of armed neutrality may have been the only thing that saved the country from foreign invasion and occupation. The Germans considered invading Sweden because they coveted the nation's factories, natural resources, and ports. The Allies considered invading to establish a staging point for a further invasion of German-occupied Europe. In the end, both sides decided that the wiser course of action was to maintain trade and diplomatic relations and avoid armed conflict with the well-prepared Swedish forces. Sweden was able once again to avoid a conflict that devastated much of the wider world.

Following World War II, Sweden expanded its industrial sector to supply the rebuilding of Europe, leading to Sweden becoming one of the richest countries in the world by 1960. As a result of maintaining peace and neutrality for the entire twentieth century, Sweden has achieved an enviable standard of living. Governed under a social democratic system, Swedes enjoy the many advantages of a high-tech economy and extensive social welfare system. Because Swedes see their current prosperity as being directly linked to peace, the nation is still not a member of any military alliance. However, the country is anxious to maintain solid economic and political ties with its neighbors, which led Sweden to join the European Union (EU) in 1995.

The Royal Palace in Stockholm

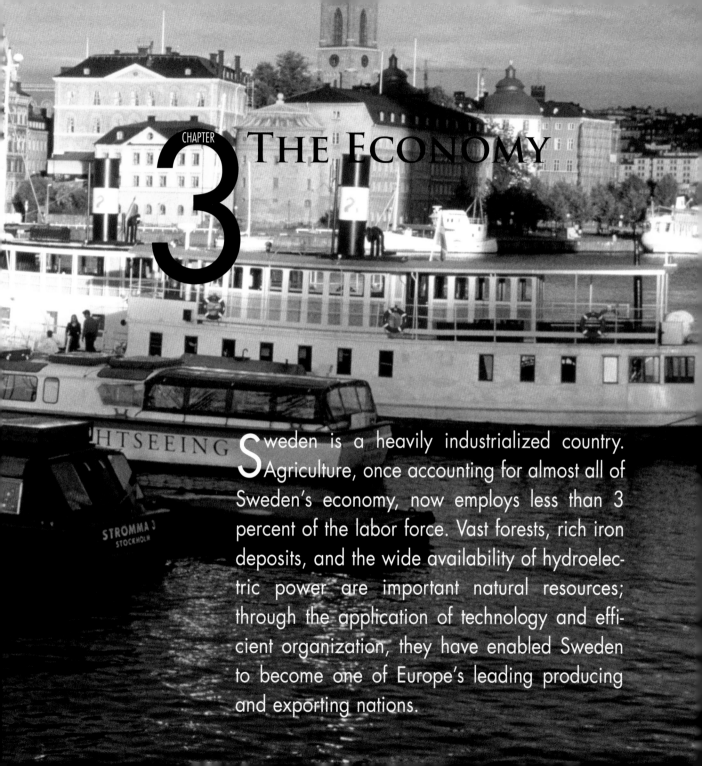

3

THE ECONOMY

Sweden is a heavily industrialized country. Agriculture, once accounting for almost all of Sweden's economy, now employs less than 3 percent of the labor force. Vast forests, rich iron deposits, and the wide availability of hydroelectric power are important natural resources; through the application of technology and efficient organization, they have enabled Sweden to become one of Europe's leading producing and exporting nations.

FORESTRY

Wood is Sweden's most important natural resource. The land is rich in timber, and many valuable coniferous softwoods are grown in Sweden, as well as a variety of less valuable hardwoods and several varieties of spruce and pine. The majority of Sweden's forests are privately owned by small farmers or form parts of larger estates, while a smaller area belongs to the state, the church, and local cooperatives. Major sawmilling and pulp corporations own the remainder of the forests. These corporate forests, which are among the best managed in the country, lie mainly in the sparsely populated north.

The annual harvest of timber in Sweden rose after World War II, from 34 million cubic meters in 1950 to 65 million cubic meters in 1971, then

Sightseeing in Stockholm

leveled off to around 52 million cubic meters in the late 1980s. Besides providing raw materials for manufacturing products such as paper, pulp, woodfiber boards, and a wide range of chemical extracts, the forests are an important source of fuel and building materials. Jobs in lumbering, the transport of timber, and the wood-processing industries employ about a quarter of a million workers. The most important timber industry is the production of planks and boards. Its output reached a peak in the early twentieth century and has remained fairly stable since the 1930s. Sawmills are located in the small ports of the Gulf of Bothnia, particularly at the mouths of the Ljungan, Indals, and Ångerman rivers. The port of Sundsvall boasts the largest concentration of wood-processing plants in the world. Sawmills located on the northern shore of Lake Vänern export cut timber through the city of Göteborg.

Timber is converted into pulp either by grinding (mechanical pulp) or by boiling and solution (chemical pulp). About 70 percent of Sweden's pulp is now produced by chemical processes. The pulp industry is concentrated mainly in the ports of southern Norrland, especially around Örnsköldsvik, and on the northern shore of Lake Vänern, where Skogshall is an important center. Sweden produced 10.1 million metric tons of pulp in 1990. The most rapidly expanding branch of the industry produces sulfate pulp.

The paper industry is located mainly in central and southern Sweden, within reach of the shipping facilities of Göteborg and the national market in Stockholm for the newspaper and publishing industries. Norrköping and Halsta have important newsprint factories. Wrapping paper and cardboard are produced in the Göta Valley and on the northern shore of Lake Vänern. Sweden is the fourth-ranking producer of newsprint in the world.

MINING

The mining of iron and copper has been important to Sweden since the Middle Ages. An enormously rich copper mine at Falun in the Bergslagen region was mined continuously for more than 650 years, until it was almost exhausted. In 1991, Sweden stood ninth among the world producers of iron ore, of which it mined 19.3 million metric tons. Until the last quarter of the nineteenth century, the main iron mines were those in Bergslagen, but today the main source of iron ore is the remote northernmost part of Norrland. For the last century, the Norwegian ice-free port of Narvik has handled a majority of exports of Swedish ore. Swedish iron ores are extremely pure, with a phosphorus content of less than 0.3 percent. Bergslagen supplies most of the ore for iron and steel manufacturing. Its most important mining center, Grängesberg, supplies the integrated iron and steel plant at Oxelösund on the Baltic coast.

Sweden ranked fifteenth among world copper producers in 1991. A new copper deposit was found in the early 1900s along the Skellefte River in Norrland. The main centers of copper mining are at Kristineberg, Boliden, and Adak, with some production still in Bergslagen. Zinc, of which Sweden also ranked ninth in world production in 1991, comes from a number of sites in both the north and south. Nickel, lead, silver, and gold are also mined in Sweden. Large uranium deposits supply the nation's nuclear power industry.

INDUSTRY: THE MAINSTAY OF ECONOMY AND EXPORTS

Swedish manufacturing employs roughly 890,000 people. Metallurgy and engineering employ 48 percent of all manufacturing workers. The timber, pulp, and paper industries follow with 21 percent, the food and beverage industry with 9 percent, and the chemical industry with 8 percent.

The production of iron and steel is one of Sweden's vital industries. This industry is located mainly in Bergslagen. These modern iron and steel plants use the latest electrical smelting processes that eliminate some of the harmful by-products of past manufacturing processes. The largest iron and steel works is at Domnarvet.

QUICK FACTS: THE ECONOMY OF SWEDEN

Gross Domestic Product (GDP): US$255.4 billion
GDP per capita: US$28,400
Industries: iron and steel, precision equipment (bearings, radio and television parts, armaments), wood pulp and paper products, processed foods, motor vehicles
Agriculture: barley, wheat, sugar beets, meat, milk
Export commodities: machinery, motor vehicles, paper products, pulp and wood, iron and steel products, chemicals
Export partners: US 10.7%, Germany 10.3%, UK 7.2%, Denmark 6.6%, Norway 6.2%, Finland 5.9%, Netherlands 4.8%, France 4.7%
Import commodities: machinery, petroleum and petroleum products, chemicals, motor vehicles, iron and steel; foodstuffs, clothing
Import partners: Germany 20.2%, Denmark 8.2%, UK 7.9%, Netherlands 7.2%, Finland 7%, France 6.1%, Belgium 4.5%
Currency: Swedish krona (SEK)
Currency exchange rate: US$1 = 6.74 SEK (December 20, 2004)

Note: All figures are from 2004.
Source: www.cia.gov, 2005.

Stockholm's busy streets

Two large plants are also located near the coast, allowing the easy import of scrap metal, as well as the export of goods for engineering industries in other parts of Sweden and the port cities of northern Europe.

Engineering is the oldest and most highly developed manufacturing industry in Scandinavia. In Sweden, it accounts for about 40 percent of the total exports and produces a wide range of products, including machinery, tools, precision gauges, electrical generating equipment, ball bearings, automobiles, and military aircraft. Various engineering centers are scattered throughout the central lowlands between Stockholm and Göteborg.

CHAPTER THREE—THE ECONOMY

The plants are often set in regional clusters, particularly around the shores of Lake Mälaren and in the Göta Valley. Malmö and the towns of southwestern Skåne are other important hubs of engineering industry.

Sweden was a dominant shipbuilding force for half a century, until this industry went into rapid decline in the late 1970s. A glut of ships on the world market (particularly of oil tankers), two international recessions, and fierce competition from low-wage countries like South Korea and Brazil have caused the total output of Swedish shipyards to fall dramatically.

AGRICULTURE

Agriculture has declined dramatically in importance in Sweden during the twentieth century. A basic feature of Swedish farming today is the widespread abandonment of land and the concentration of agriculture in the most favorable areas of the country. As small farms became deserted when their owners grew old and died, the government has intervened to compel the **amalgamation** of the property into larger units. Consequently, the number of small, privately owned farms has declined from 96,000 in 1951 to 15,000 in 1990.

Although only about 3 percent of the labor force held agricultural jobs in 1990, compared with 29 percent in 1940, agricultural output has not declined. In fact, modern technology has led to an increase in output despite the reduced area of farmland. Field drains, striking experiments in plant breeding for northern latitudes, widespread use of fertilizers, cooperatives for marketing agricultural commodities, and **dissemination** of technical information on farming have all contributed to increased harvests.

As in the other Scandinavian countries, the principal agricultural activity in Sweden is raising livestock. Because of the importance of livestock, three-quarters of the land under cultivation is devoted to fodder crops. More than half of this area is devoted to growing rotation grass, a fast-growing combination of rye grass, timothy, and clover. Most of this grass is converted into hay for the indoor feeding of livestock in winter, which lasts from five to seven months. Cereals are the second-most important crop. The main wheat-producing areas are the central lowlands and Skåne, though spring wheat is grown at favorable sites in Norrland's valleys as far north as the Arctic Circle. Rye and oats grow extensively on the western coastal plains. Barley is an important fodder crop in southwest Skåne.

Due to the long decline in its relative economic importance, Swedish government programs of price supports and incentives has sustained the country's agricultural sector. Swedish agricultural policy had as its goal the maintenance of an 80 percent level of self-sufficiency for farms providing basic foodstuffs. However, subsidies have been significantly cut back in recent years.

ENERGY SOURCES

In the 1960s and 1970s, the Swedish government devoted major resources to the development of its

A busy restaurant in Stockholm

The world's largest ferries dock at Sodermalm Pier

nuclear generating capacity, making Sweden, with twelve nuclear power plants, by far the world's largest per capita producer of nuclear energy. A referendum in 1980 overwhelmingly endorsed phasing out nuclear power by 2010, but the plan was put on hold in 1990. In that year, nuclear power provided 51 percent of the nation's electricity, at one of the lowest per-unit costs in the world.

Hydroelectric power has also played an important role in economic development throughout Scandinavia. By 1990, hydroelectric production in Sweden was 72.2 billion kilowatt hours, an amount surpassed in Europe only by Norway. Almost two-thirds of the country's hydroelectric potential has been utilized. However, for environmental reasons, no new rivers may be dammed unless alternative energy sources prove too expensive. The majority of the country's waterpower comes from long, powerful rivers in Norrland, while the chief area of consumption is in the cities of the central lowlands and the south. Thus, one of the main problems in the use of hydroelectric power has been the development of economical means of transmission over long distances.

TRANSPORTATION

Domestic freight in Sweden is moved mainly by road and rail. Trucks carry about half the nation's freight. State-built railroads are the principal means of commercial transport and carry one-third of the nation's freight and dominate long-distance hauling; they also move ores within the north. Shipping, chiefly of construction materials, accounts for about one-sixth of the freight. Sweden's merchant fleet was less than 4 million gross registered tons in 1980, and half that in 1990. Oil tankers accounted for about half the tonnage. Göteborg has the largest import trade, and Luleå the largest export trade. Sweden has a number of other ports of regional importance, including Stockholm, Malmö, and Norrköping. About 90 percent of the passenger traffic is by car and bus. In 1990, there was one car for every 2.4 persons in Sweden.

SWEDEN'S ECONOMY TODAY

Modern Sweden is one of the most highly industrialized countries in the world. It is the industrial giant of Scandinavia. The nation's early economic growth was built upon a combination of state-owned industries, consumer and producer cooperatives, and privately held companies.

Private ownership of corporations is somewhat more limited in Sweden than in other advanced nations. In the early 1990s, fourteen corporations dominated the Swedish economy; three of them accounted for about two-thirds of all private-sector sales and employees. Privatization of state-owned industries and the move toward EU antitrust standards and foreign ownership are being implemented gradually. As this happens, it is expected to result in increased foreign investment and continuing economic growth. The future for the Swedish economy continues to look bright.

Windsurfing in Stockholm

4 SWEDEN'S PEOPLE AND CULTURE

The population of Sweden was estimated at 9,001,774 in 2005. This gives the country an overall population density of fifty-seven persons per square mile (22 per square kilometer). Although Sweden as a whole is sparsely populated, regional population densities can vary greatly. The great majority of the population lives in the southern third of Sweden, especially in the central lowlands, the plains of Skåne, and coastal areas. Population is the densest around the cities of Stockholm, Göteborg, and Malmö. Large areas of the north are especially sparsely inhabited. Sweden is also highly urbanized, with more than 80 percent of Swedes living in the nation's cities.

Ethnically, Sweden consists mainly of Scandinavians of Germanic descent. Due to a dramatic increase in immigration, Sweden's ethnic diversity has grown rapidly in recent decades. For many years, Sweden was a nation of emigrants. From 1860 to World War I, more than one million Swedes left the country, mainly for the United States. Emigration declined significantly after 1930, as the nation grew more prosperous. Following World War II, Sweden welcomed many refugees and other displaced people. Since then, immigration has accounted for nearly half of Sweden's population growth. Today, approximately 20 percent of the population are immigrants or have at least one foreign-born parent. Many of these immigrants have come to Sweden as political refugees.

The largest immigrant groups in Sweden are from neighboring Scandinavian countries. About 17,000 ethnic Saami live mainly in the far north, although in recent decades many Saami have migrated south, mainly to Stockholm. Sweden is also home to large numbers of immigrants who fled the conflict in the former Yugoslavia, especially from Serbia and Montenegro, and Bosnia and Herzegovina. In fact, only Germany has received more refugees from that region. Other important immigrant groups include people from Iran, Iraq, Hungary, Turkey, and Poland.

RELIGION: FREEDOM OF CHOICE

The Swedish constitution guarantees freedom of religion. Approximately 80 percent of the population belongs to the Church of Sweden. It is possible to leave the Church of Sweden, and an increasing number of persons do so. In 1999, the Church of Sweden and the State separated, and, as a result, more than twice as many people left the church in that year as compared to previous years.

While weekly services in Christian houses of worship are usually poorly attended, a large number of persons observe major festivals of the church and prefer a religious ceremony to mark the turning points of life. Approximately 70 percent of children are baptized, 40 percent of those eligible are confirmed, and 90 percent of funeral services are performed under the auspices of the Church of Sweden. Approximately 60 percent of couples marrying choose a Church of Sweden ceremony.

Sweden has several smaller Christian faith communities as well. The Roman Catholic Church and the Russian Orthodox Church are represented. Several small churches are offshoots of nineteenth-century revival movements in the Church of Sweden. Others, such as the Baptist Union of Sweden and the Methodist Church of Sweden, trace their roots to British and North American protestant movements.

The Jewish community has 10,000 active members; however, the total number of Jews living in the country is estimated to be approximately 20,000. There are Orthodox, Conservative, and Reform Jewish synagogues.

The major religious communities and the Church of Sweden are spread across the country. In recent decades, the large influx of immigrants has led to the introduction of nontraditional religions in their new communities. Islam is a growing religion in Sweden. The Muslim community has

Churches in Sweden are used primarily for ceremonies marking life's major events.

Twin-spired Vaxjo Cathedral in Smaland

approximately 350,000 members; approximately 100,000 of those are active. Muslim affiliations represented by immigrant groups are predominantly the Shiite and Sunni branches of Islam. Buddhists and Hindus number approximately 3,000 to 4,000 persons each. The Church of Jesus Christ of Latter-day Saints (Mormons) and other foreign missionary groups are active throughout the country. Approximately 15 percent of the adult population is atheist.

FOOD AND DRINK: SMÖRGÅSBORD

Swedish food is usually simple and satisfying, and nowadays also healthy. In the last few decades, immigrants from all over the world have enriched Sweden's food culture with a host of exciting dishes. Foreign fast food, for example, has become an inseparable part of Swedish youth culture.

The feature of Swedish cuisine most familiar to foreigners is the smörgåsbord. Though the word smörgås means "open sandwich," and bord is the Swedish word for "table," a smörgåsbord is not a table full of sandwiches. Instead, this specialty consists of a number of small dishes from which you can take your pick. A typical smörgåsbord usually contains a number of herring dishes, Swedish meatballs,

QUICK FACTS: THE PEOPLE OF SWEDEN

Population: 9,001,774

Ethnic groups: indigenous population: Swedes and Finnish and Saami minorities; foreign-born or first-generation immigrants: Finns, Yugoslavs, Danes, Norwegians, Greeks, Turks

Age structure:
   0–14 years: 17.1%
   15–64 years: 65.5%
   65 years and over: 17.4%

Population growth rate: 0.17%

Birth rate: 10.36 births/1,000 pop.

Death rate: 10.36 deaths/1,000 pop.

Migration rate: 1.67 migrant(s)/1,000 pop.

Infant mortality rate: 2.77 deaths/1,000 live births

Life expectancy at birth:
   Total population: 80.4 years
   Male: 78.19 years
   Female: 82.74 years

Total fertility rate: 1.66 children born/woman

Religions: Lutheran 87%, Roman Catholic, Orthodox, Baptist, Muslim, Jewish, Buddhist

Languages: Swedish, with small Sami- and Finnish-speaking minorities

Literacy rate: 99% (1979)

Note: All figures are from 2005 unless otherwise noted.
Source: www.cia.gov, 2005.

A typical Swedish meal includes salmon.

salmon, pies, salads, "Jansson's temptation" (sliced herring, potatoes, and onions baked in cream), eggs, bread, and some kind of potato dish. Smörgåsbord was originally served in the eighteenth century as an appetizer before the main course. Today, however, it has become a meal in itself. Few people ask for more after having tried everything on a smörgåsbord!

THE WELFARE STATE: THE "HOME OF THE PEOPLE"

Home to the world's highest tax burden, Sweden has created what is often called the world's most generous general social welfare system, with such elements as virtually free (that is, tax-financed) education, child care, health care, pensions, elder care, social services, and various social security systems.

Although Sweden has always had a solid market economy, the Social Democratic Party that ran the government for most of the twentieth century borrowed many ideas from **socialism**. Swedish wealth has been redistributed among the population to a greater extent than in perhaps any other country. "From each according to ability, to each according to needs" is the basic philosophy of socialism; all people are guaranteed economic security in all stages of life.

This welfare state, known in Sweden as the "home of the people," was a unique experiment in social engineering that has attracted great attention worldwide. Other countries have copied many of its features. In recent decades, as the country's previous economic growth has stalled, the Swedish welfare state has been under heavy pressures. Today, the country's social security systems are financially burdened and are struggling with serious structural problems. The recent flood of poor refugees and immigrants has increased the drain on the welfare system, and since joining the EU in 1995, the Swedish government has been under outside pressure to bring its welfare programs in line with those of the other EU member states. Yet the main features of the Swedish welfare state, with its guaranteed and publicly financed safety net for the entire population, has remained largely untouched—so far.

Stockholm, Sweden's capital city

5 THE CITIES

CHAPTER

Today's Sweden is heavily urbanized, with more than 80 percent of the nation's people living in and around urban areas. As a result, the rest of Sweden is thinly populated, giving the country one of the lowest population densities in Europe. Sweden's three largest and most important cities are Stockholm, the capital; Göteborg; and Malmö. Other major cities include Uppsala, Linköping, Örebro, Norrköping, and Västerås.

STOCKHOLM: THE CAPITAL

Stockholm had a population of 761,721 in 2004. The city is often compared to Venice because of its scenic bridges and waterways and its historic architecture. Located in east-central Sweden, the city is built on about twenty islands and a narrow strip of land between Lake Mälaran and the Baltic Sea. Stockholm is famous for its historic quarter, the Old Town (Gamla Stan), located on three central islands in the city's harbor. Old Town is home to the magnificent Royal Palace, Stockholm's city hall (the Stadshuset), and the Great Church, a part of which dates to the thirteenth century. Stockholm is Sweden's financial, commercial, cultural, and administrative center.

GÖTEBORG: A RICH METROPOLIS

Göteborg, Sweden's second-largest city is located on the Kattegat, the strait separating Sweden from Denmark. The city has a tremendous harbor, the largest in Scandinavia, and is the country's leading port. Göteborg is a critical transportation hub on the Göta Canal, and is home to a large international airport. Despite being hard-hit by the decline of the Swedish shipbuilding industry, Göteborg remains an important industrial city with factories producing automobiles, automobile parts, and telecommunications equipment. It is also a center for banking and financial services, medical research and pharmaceuticals, and information technology. The city also boasts the famous Göteborg Botanical Garden and Liseburg, the largest amusement park in Scandinavia and one of Sweden's most popular tourist attractions.

MALMÖ: A TRANSPORTATION HUB

Malmö is Sweden's third-largest city. It is home to one of Sweden's major ports and is also a rail, air, and highway hub. Malmö is the headquarters of Sweden's pharmaceuticals industry, and its modern fiber optic cable networks support a vigorous information technology sector. In 2000, an important bridge and tunnel opened, connecting Malmö with Copenhagen, Denmark. Copenhagen, once accessible only by air or sea, is located just fifteen miles (24 kilometers) across Öresund strait. The new bridge, called the Øresundsbron, makes it possible to travel between Sweden and Denmark in just fifteen minutes.

UPPSALA: A CENTER FOR RESEARCH AND EDUCATION

Uppsala is Sweden's fourth-largest city. Perhaps best known for its university, founded in the fifteenth century, the city also offers visitors beautiful surroundings, a lively cultural scene, and a wealth of historic architecture. Today, Uppsala is a vibrant industrial and commercial city. At Uppsala University, extensive research is carried out in a number of fields to promote the development of industry, commerce, and entrepreneurship. Uppsala is also Scandinavia's leading medical center. The country's only pharmacy and veterinary medicine colleges can be found here.

The National Museum in Sweden

LINKÖPING: A HISTORIC GEM

Linköping, Sweden's fifth-largest city, has an ancient history as County Town, as a military city, and as a center of learning. Historic Linköping Castle now accommodates the home of the county governor. The Castle and Cathedral Museum is a prominent tourist attraction. Next to the castle and the cathedral is the old church Latin School for Boys, which was the first school in Linköping. The city is now recognized as an important city of learning. Today, Linköping is a dynamic university town and a center of commerce. Economic development began to expand when Saab located its aircraft manufacturing facilities here in 1937.

The EU flag

6

THE FORMATION OF THE EUROPEAN UNION

The EU is an economic and political confederation of twenty-five European nations. Member countries abide by common foreign and security policies and cooperate on judicial and domestic affairs. The confederation, however, does not replace existing states or governments. Each of the twenty-five member states is **autonomous**, but they have all agreed to establish some common institutions and to hand over some of their own decision-making powers to these international bodies. As a result, decisions on matters that interest all member states can be made democratically, accommodating everyone's concerns and interests.

Today, the EU is the most powerful regional organization in the world. It has evolved from a primarily economic organization to an increasingly political one. Besides promoting economic cooperation, the EU requires that its members uphold fundamental values of peace and **solidarity**, human dignity, freedom, and equality. Based on the principles of democracy and the rule of law, the EU respects the culture and organizations of member states.

HISTORY

The seeds of the EU were planted more than fifty years ago in a Europe reduced to smoking piles of rubble by two world wars. European nations suffered great financial difficulties in the postwar period. They were struggling to get back on their feet and realized that another war would cause further hardship. Knowing that internal conflict was hurting all of Europe, a drive began toward European cooperation.

France took the first historic step. On May 9, 1950 (now celebrated as Europe Day), Robert Schuman, the French foreign minister, proposed the coal and steel industries of France and West Germany be coordinated under a single supranational authority. The proposal, known as the Treaty

of Paris, attracted four other countries—Belgium, Luxembourg, the Netherlands, and Italy—and resulted in the 1951 formation of the European Coal and Steel Community (ECSC). These six countries became the founding members of the EU.

In 1957, European cooperation took its next big leap. Under the Treaty of Rome, the European Economic Community (EEC) and the European Atomic Energy Community (EURATOM) were formed. Informally known as the Common Market, the EEC promoted joining the national economies into a single European economy. The 1965 Treaty of Brussels (more commonly referred to as the Merger Treaty) united these various treaty organizations under a single umbrella, the European Community (EC).

In 1992, the Maastricht Treaty (also known as the Treaty of the European Union) was signed in Maastricht, the Netherlands, signaling the birth of the EU as it stands today. **Ratified** the following year, the Maastricht Treaty provided for a central banking system, a common currency (the euro) to replace the national currencies, a legal definition of the EU, and a framework for expanding the

The EU's united economy has allowed it to become a worldwide financial power.

EU's political role, particularly in the area of foreign and security policy.

By 1993, the member countries completed their move toward a single market and agreed to participate in a larger common market, the European Economic Area, established in 1994.

The EU, headquartered in Brussels, Belgium, reached its current member strength in spurts. In

© BCE ECB EZB EKT EKP 2002

© BCE ECB EZB EKT EKP 2002

© BCE ECB EZB EKT EKP 2002

© BCE ECB EZB EKT EKP 2002

The euro, the EU's currency

1973, Denmark, Ireland, and the United Kingdom joined the six founding members of the EC. They were followed by Greece in 1981, and Portugal and Spain in 1986. The 1990s saw the unification of the two Germanys, and as a result, East Germany entered the EU fold. Austria, Finland, and Sweden joined the EU in 1995, bringing the total number of member states to fifteen. In 2004, the EU nearly doubled its size when ten countries—Cyprus, the Czech Republic, Estonia, Hungary, Latvia, Lithuania, Malta, Poland, Slovakia, and Slovenia—became members.

THE EU FRAMEWORK

The EU's structure has often been compared to a "roof of a temple with three columns." As established by the Maastricht Treaty, this three-pillar framework encompasses all the policy areas—or pillars—of European cooperation. The three pillars of the EU are the European Community, the Common Foreign and Security Policy (CFSP), and Police and Judicial Co-operation in Criminal Matters.

QUICK FACTS: THE EUROPEAN UNION

Number of Member Countries: 25
Official Languages: 20—Czech, Danish, Dutch, English, Estonian, Finnish, French, German, Greek, Hungarian, Italian, Latvian, Lithuanian, Maltese, Polish, Portuguese, Slovak, Slovenian, Spanish, and Swedish; additional language for treaty purposes: Irish Gaelic
Motto: *In Varietate Concordia* (United in Diversity)
European Council's President: Each member state takes a turn to lead the council's activities for 6 months.
European Commission's President: José Manuel Barroso (Portugal)
European Parliament's President: Josep Borrell (Spain)
Total Area: 1,502,966 square miles (3,892,685 sq. km.)
Population: 454,900,000
Population Density: 302.7 people/square mile (116.8 people/sq. km.)
GDP: €9.61.1012
Per Capita GDP: €21,125
Formation:
- Declared: February 7, 1992, with signing of the Maastricht Treaty
- Recognized: November 1, 1993, with the ratification of the Maastricht Treaty

Community Currency: Euro. Currently 12 of the 25 member states have adopted the euro as their currency.
Anthem: "Ode to Joy"
Flag: Blue background with 12 gold stars arranged in a circle
Official Day: Europe Day, May 9

Source: europa.eu.int

PILLAR ONE

The European Community pillar deals with economic, social, and environmental policies. It is a body consisting of the European Parliament, European Commission, European Court of Justice, Council of the European Union, and the European Courts of Auditors.

PILLAR TWO

The idea that the EU should speak with one voice in world affairs is as old as the European integration process itself. Toward this end, the Common Foreign and Security Policy (CFSP) was formed in 1993.

PILLAR THREE

The cooperation of EU member states in judicial and criminal matters ensures that its citizens enjoy the freedom to travel, work, and live securely and safely anywhere within the EU. The third pillar—Police and Judicial Co-operation in Criminal Matters—helps to protect EU citizens from international crime and to ensure equal access to justice and fundamental rights across the EU.

The flags of the EU's nations:

top row, left to right
Belgium, the Czech Republic, Denmark, Germany, Estonia, Greece

second row, left to right
Spain, France, Ireland, Italy, Cyprus, Latvia

third row, left to right
Lithuania, Luxembourg, Hungary, Malta, the Netherlands, Austria

bottom row, left to right
Poland, Portugal, Slovenia, Slovakia, Finland, Sweden, United Kingdom

ECONOMIC STATUS

As of May 2004, the EU had the largest economy in the world, followed closely by the United States. But even though the EU continues to enjoy a trade surplus, it faces the twin problems of high unemployment rates and **stagnancy**.

The 2004 addition of ten new member states is expected to boost economic growth. EU membership is likely to stimulate the economies of these relatively poor countries. In turn, their prosperity growth will be beneficial to the EU.

THE EURO

The EU's official currency is the euro, which came into circulation on January 1, 2002. The shift to the euro has been the largest monetary changeover in the world. Twelve countries—Belgium, Germany, Greece, Spain, France, Ireland, Italy, Luxembourg, the Netherlands, Finland, Portugal, and Austria—have adopted it as their currency.

SINGLE MARKET

Within the EU, laws of member states are harmonized and domestic policies are coordinated to create a larger, more-efficient single market.

The chief features of the EU's internal policy on the single market are:

- free trade of goods and services

- a common EU competition law that controls anticompetitive activities of companies and member states

- removal of internal border control and harmonization of external controls between member states

- freedom for citizens to live and work anywhere in the EU as long as they are not dependent on the state

- free movement of **capital** between member states

- harmonization of government regulations, corporation law, and trademark registration

- a single currency

- coordination of environmental policy

- a common agricultural policy and a common fisheries policy

- a common system of indirect taxation, the value-added tax (VAT), and common customs duties and **excise**

- funding for research

- funding for aid to disadvantaged regions

The EU's external policy on the single market specifies:

- a common external **tariff** and a common position in international trade negotiations

- funding of programs in other Eastern European countries and developing countries

COOPERATION AREAS

EU member states cooperate in other areas as well. Member states can vote in European Parliament elections. Intelligence sharing and cooperation in criminal matters are carried out through EUROPOL and the Schengen Information System.

The EU is working to develop common foreign and security policies. Many member states are resisting such a move, however, saying these are sensitive areas best left to individual member states. Arguing in favor of a common approach to security and foreign policy are countries like France and Germany, who insist that a safer and more secure Europe can only become a reality under the EU umbrella.

One of the EU's great achievements has been to create a boundary-free area within which people, goods, services, and money can move around freely; this ease of movement is sometimes called "the four freedoms." As the EU grows in size, so do the challenges facing it—and yet its fifty-year history has amply demonstrated the power of cooperation.

Europe is proud of its "bright idea," a union with economic and political power.

The EU believes that it can use its power to act as a "lighthouse" for the rest of the world.

KEY EU INSTITUTIONS

Five key institutions play a specific role in the EU.

THE EUROPEAN PARLIAMENT

The European Parliament (EP) is the democratic voice of the people of Europe. Directly elected every five years, the Members of the European Parliament (MEPs) sit not in national **blocs** but in political groups representing the seven main political parties of the member states. Each group reflects the political ideology of the national parties to which its members belong. Some MEPs are not attached to any political group.

COUNCIL OF THE EUROPEAN UNION

The Council of the European Union (formerly known as the Council of Ministers) is the main leg-

islative and decision-making body in the EU. It brings together the nationally elected representatives of the member-state governments. One minister from each of the EU's member states attends council meetings. It is the forum in which government representatives can assert their interests and reach compromises. Increasingly, the Council of the European Union and the EP are acting together as colegislators in decision-making processes.

EUROPEAN COMMISSION

The European Commission does much of the day-to-day work of the EU. Politically independent, the commission represents the interests of the EU as a whole, rather than those of individual member states. It drafts proposals for new European laws, which it presents to the EP and the Council of the European Union. The European Commission makes sure EU decisions are implemented properly and supervises the way EU funds are spent. It also sees that everyone abides by the European treaties and European law.

The EU member-state governments choose the European Commission president, who is then approved by the EP. Member states, in consultation with the incoming president, nominate the other European Commission members, who must also be approved by the EP. The commission is appointed for a five-year term, but can be dismissed by the EP. Many members of its staff work in Brussels, Belgium.

COURT OF JUSTICE

Headquartered in Luxembourg, the Court of Justice of the European Communities consists of one independent judge from each EU country. This court ensures that the common rules decided in the EU are understood and followed uniformly by all the members. The Court of Justice settles disputes over how EU treaties and legislation are interpreted. If national courts are in doubt about how to apply EU rules, they must ask the Court of Justice. Individuals can also bring proceedings against EU institutions before the court.

COURT OF AUDITORS

EU funds must be used legally, economically, and for their intended purpose. The Court of Auditors, an independent EU institution located in Luxembourg, is responsible for overseeing how EU money is spent. In effect, these auditors help European taxpayers get better value for the money that has been channeled into the EU.

OTHER IMPORTANT BODIES

1. European Economic and Social Committee: expresses the opinions of organized civil society on economic and social issues

2. Committee of the Regions: expresses the opinions of regional and local authorities

3. European Central Bank: responsible for monetary policy and managing the euro

4. European Ombudsman: deals with citizens' complaints about mismanagement by any EU institution or body

5. European Investment Bank: helps achieve EU objectives by financing investment projects

Together with a number of agencies and other bodies completing the system, the EU's institutions have made it the most powerful organization in the world.

EU MEMBER STATES

In order to become a member of the EU, a country must have a stable democracy that guarantees the rule of law, human rights, and protection of minorities. It must also have a functioning market economy as well as a civil service capable of applying and managing EU laws.

The EU provides substantial financial assistance and advice to help candidate countries prepare themselves for membership. As of October 2004, the EU has twenty-five member states. Bulgaria and Romania are likely to join in 2007, which would bring the EU's total population to nearly 500 million.

In December 2004, the EU decided to open negotiations with Turkey on its proposed membership. Turkey's possible entry into the EU has been fraught with controversy. Much of this controversy has centered on Turkey's human rights record and the divided island of Cyprus. If allowed to join the EU, Turkey would be its most-populous member state.

The 2004 expansion was the EU's most ambitious enlargement to date. Never before has the EU embraced so many new countries, grown so much in terms of area and population, or encompassed so many different histories and cultures. As the EU moves forward into the twenty-first century, it will undoubtedly continue to grow in both political and economic strength.

A quiet street in Stockholm

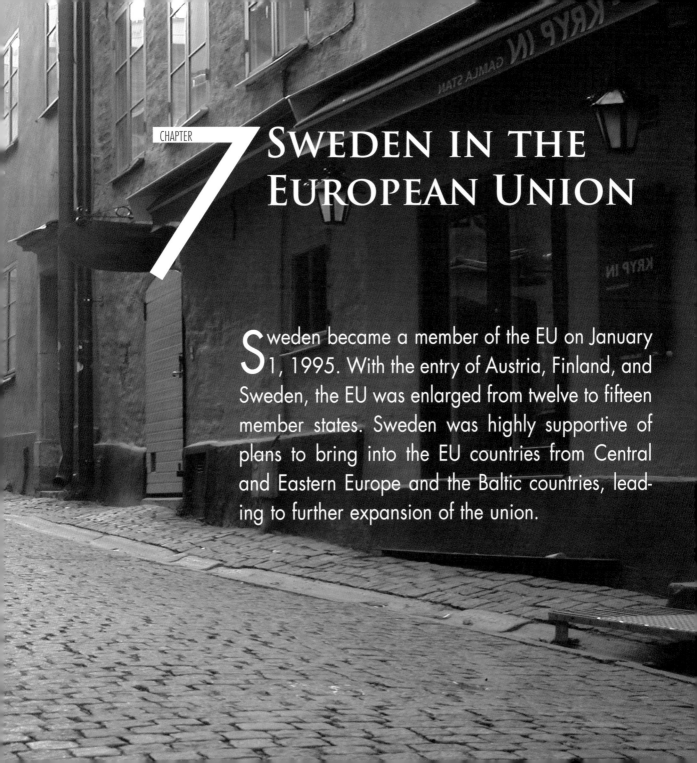

7 SWEDEN IN THE EUROPEAN UNION

Sweden became a member of the EU on January 1, 1995. With the entry of Austria, Finland, and Sweden, the EU was enlarged from twelve to fifteen member states. Sweden was highly supportive of plans to bring into the EU countries from Central and Eastern Europe and the Baltic countries, leading to further expansion of the union.

Greater openness, strengthened environmental commitments, and more intensive measures to counteract unemployment are priority issues for Sweden in the work of the EU.

SWEDEN'S PLACE IN EU HISTORY

In 1960, Denmark, Norway, Portugal, Sweden, Switzerland, Austria, and the United Kingdom created the European Free Trade Association (EFTA). They were later joined by Finland, Liechtenstein, and Iceland; today, only Iceland, Norway, Switzerland, and Liechtenstein remain members. EFTA provided a means of lowering barriers to free trade between these nations and was an opportunity for Sweden to demonstrate its openness to greater international cooperation.

In the late 1960s and early 1970s, Sweden negotiated closer ties with the EU's predecessor, the European Community or EC. This was done as an "open application," which was not the same as full membership. However, membership was regarded as increasingly unlikely because Sweden insisted on maintaining their policy of neutrality. In 1972, Sweden and the EC settled an agreement on free trade. This came into force in 1973 and included primarily industrial products. Similar bilateral agreements were signed between other EFTA member states and the EC.

The abolition of all customs tariffs for industrial goods between Sweden and the EC was completed in 1984. At that time, the EC and EFTA agreed to further extend their cooperation. In 1987, Sweden expressed a wish to join the internal market of the EC, and by 1989, the EC and EFTA had initiated talks on the creation of a European economic area of cooperation, the European Economic Area (EEA). The purpose of this body was to achieve the free movement of goods, persons, services, and capital and to cooperate within certain limited areas such as consumer protection, research and development, and education.

In 1990, formal negotiations on an EEA agreement began in Brussels. The Swedish government announced that its goal was that country's membership in the EU. Sweden formally applied for EU membership in in 1991. The EEA agreement was signed in 1992 and went into effect January 1, 1994. In 1993, Sweden entered into formal negotiations for EU membership. By 1994, these membership negotiations were concluded, and an agreement was signed in June at the European Council meeting on Korfu. In November of the same year, the Swedish people voiced their approval of EU membership in a referendum, although the measure passed by a very slight margin. Sweden formally joined the EU in 1995.

Swedish Opinion of the EU

Attitudes toward EU membership are fairly positive in Sweden. This was demonstrated by a study done in September 2000 by the Swedish Ministry for Foreign Affairs. The study showed that there are more positive attitudes toward EU membership than there are negative. Replying to the question, "Do you think that it is positive or negative that Sweden is a member of the EU?" 44 percent of people responded that it was positive; 39 percent felt that it was negative, and the remaining 17 percent replied that they did not know.

Stockholm's harbor serves all of Europe.

Crowded outdoor cafe in Gothenberg

When asked what people regarded as the most important issue the EU ought to address, the most common answer was environmental protection, followed by measures to counteract unemployment, resolve economic issues, and maintain peace and cooperation within the EU. The study also illustrated the extent to which the Swedish general public considered that the EU should be responsible for each of eleven specific areas, and the extent to which they felt that the EU met that

responsibility. The greatest differences between public expectations and EU actions were in areas relating to combating the spread of hate crimes, fighting international crime, taking a collective responsibility for refugees in Europe, gender equality issues, and full employment.

According to the same study, three out of five Swedes keep themselves educated about what the EU stands for and what it is working on. The most common sources of information are the daily newspapers and television news programs. About half of all Swedes think that information currently given on the EU functions well for them. Four of ten Swedes feel the need for more information. The Swedish people are well educated and highly literate, and although a majority of people feel EU membership has improved life in Sweden, there is still a sizable minority who is unhappy with the level of independence Sweden has surrendered to the EU. In general, Swedes are distrustful of any measures originating from Brussels that are perceived as a threat to Swedish **sovereignty**.

THE EU AND SWEDISH CONCERNS

Negotiations between Sweden and the EU were extensive as Sweden prepared for **accession**. Because of the nation's long history of military neutrality and their many distinct laws and customs, the Swedes were determined that EU membership would not override the wishes of the Swedish voting public. As a result, Sweden has established many areas where domestic policies rather that those established in Brussels will take precedence.

First and foremost, Sweden retains its neutrality. This was a nonnegotiable Swedish condition during the membership process. However, Sweden supports efforts to strengthen the EU's capacity for conflict prevention as well as civil and military crisis management. Sweden is also willing to participate in European peacekeeping activities and humanitarian efforts.

Another important Swedish demand was that the country would not have to lower its environmental standards in areas where its laws were stricter than those proposed by the EU. Sweden is allowed to keep its own laws while waiting for the EU to move closer to Swedish standards. Meanwhile, the EU has conducted a review of its environmental rules, including those for cadmium, arsenic, and various chemicals. As a result, the transitional period has been used in order to change or initiate changes in EU rules.

Sweden contributes to the common EU budget in proportion to the size of the country. Sweden

Sweden is famous for its glass.

demanded, and received, the right to pay a reduced contribution over the first four years. Sweden also considered it important for the EU to acknowledge that cold, sparsely populated areas of northern Europe are entitled to regional subsidies. The outcome of the negotiations was that the EU introduced a new type of regional aid for areas with population densities below eight inhabitants per square kilometer. Almost half of Sweden is entitled to this special EU assistance. In addition, Sweden was able to access a portion of existing regional subsidies from the EU. These subsidies have gone primarily to less developed, thinly populated portions of the country. These funds have helped improve the infrastructure of many of the nation's most isolated and rural areas.

Like other EU countries, Sweden has a number of traditions and customs it did not wish to give up in order to join the EU. The Swedish have a widespread habit of using moist snuff (placing smokeless tobacco in the mouth) and were guaranteed the right to continue this practice, even though this product is banned in the other EU member states. Another issue important to Sweden during its EU membership negotiations was the right to continue operating Systembolaget, the government-owned company that maintains a monopoly on retail sales of beer, wine, and liquor to the general public. Sweden persuaded the EU to allow the continuation of Systembolaget's retail monopoly. Meanwhile, the previous government monopoly on importing these alcoholic beverages was abolished. Today, the importation of such alcoholic beverages is unrestricted, but they must be sold via Systembolaget.

This provision was actually challenged in the European Court of Justice in Luxembourg, which declared in its verdict that the monopoly did not violate EU rules. As long as it continues to stock a wide selection of alcoholic beverages and does not discriminate against any individual producer, Systembolaget may continue operating. The Swedes insist that the primary motive for the monopoly is for reasons of health, with alcoholic beverage sales thus being carefully controlled by Swedish law.

THE WAY FORWARD

While the Swedes continue to be fiercely protective of their sovereignty and interests, they cannot deny that the EU has greatly improved the standard of living, security, and international influence of Sweden and Europe as a whole. Continued efforts to set up a common customs union for all EU member states, reduce trade barriers, and adopt common quality standards for goods and services have begun to pay dividends for Sweden as well as the rest of Europe.

A Calendar of Swedish Festivals

Sweden celebrates many religious, historical, and nonreligious festivals. Food, fun, parades, and dancing are integral parts of most Swedish festivals.

January: January 1 is a public holiday. The **New Year** festivities traditionally include champagne and fireworks. **Epiphany Eve** and **Epiphany**, celebrated on January 5 and 6, mark the end of the Christmas season. On this holiday, children dress up as the Three Wise Men and go door to door collecting money for charity and receive candies as their reward.

March/April: Easter Week may fall in March or April, and the festival is celebrated throughout the country. In Sweden, **Easter** begins on **Maundy Thursday**, followed by **Good Friday**. Easter worship begins on Saturday evening and resumes on Sunday morning. **Easter Sunday** is a day for families to celebrate together. Swedish families enjoy a special smörgåsbord. **Easter Monday** is a day of rest and marks the final day of celebration.

May: May Day is celebrated on the eve of May 1. This festival signifies the end of winter and is accompanied by singing and dancing around the may pole in traditional clothes. **Ascension Eve**, **Ascension Day**, and **Pentecost**, religious festivals, fall in the May–June period.

June: June 6 is **National Day**, and is a patriotic celebration. **Midsummer's Eve** and **Midsummer's Day** also fall in June. In Sweden, Midsummer's Eve and Midsummer's Day were moved to the third Friday and Saturday of June, in order to make a dependable long weekend. As Midsummer is one of the times of the year when magic is believed to be strongest, it was considered a good night to perform rituals to look into the future. Today, this tradition survives, and young girls pick bouquets of seven or nine different flowers and put them under their pillow in the hope of dreaming about their future husband.

August/September: August is the month when Swedes have special parties to celebrate the crayfish and the Baltic herring. Swedes decorate their balconies and terraces with pretty lanterns and serve boiled crayfish to their friends. The crayfish season starts at midnight on the second Wednesday in August; a law forbids catching crayfish before this time.

In northern Sweden, many people like "surströmmingen," Baltic herring that has been allowed to ferment. On the third Thursday of August, the year's supply of this delicacy is first put up for sale. People have parties featuring this fish served with crackers, potatoes, chopped onions, and beer.

October/ November: October 31is **All Saint's Eve**, followed on November 1 by **All Saints' Day**. People remember and honor the dead on this day.

December: Christmas dominates this time of year. It starts with **Advent**, four Sundays before Christmas Day and ends with the **Twentieth Day of Christmas**, the day when Swedes traditionally take down their Christmas trees. A highlight of the season is **Saint Lucia Day**, December 13. This day of celebration features a very early morning visit from Sankta Lucia. All over Sweden people get up early as the household's eldest daughter, dressed in white with a wreath of candles on her head, serves everyone a cup of hot "glögg" and a Lucia bun. The Christmas festivities start with **Christmas Eve** on December 24, followed by **Christmas Day** and **Boxing Day**. Sweden completely shuts down during this time; not only are stores and businesses closed, but public transportation is cancelled.

Lussekatter
(Lucia Buns)

This classic Swedish pastry is traditionally served on St. Lucia Day.

Yields 12 buns

Ingredients
1/3 cup milk
1/4 cup butter or margarine
1/4 cup warm water
1 package yeast
1/4 cup sugar
1 egg
1/2 teaspoon salt
1/4 teaspoon saffron
2 3/4 cups flour
vegetable oil
1 egg
1 tablespoon water
raisins

Directions
Combine the milk and butter or margarine in a small saucepan, and heat until the butter or margarine melts. Mix the warm water and yeast in a large bowl. Add the warm milk mixture. Add the egg, sugar, salt, and saffron. Add 1 and 1/2 cups of flour and mix well. Gradually add more flour until the dough is stiff. Knead the dough on a floured surface for 5 to 10 minutes. Coat a large bowl with cooking oil and put in the dough. Cover with a towel and let the dough rise in a warm location until it has doubled in size.

After the dough has doubled, punch it down. Divide it into 12 sections, rolling each section into a rope. Cross two ropes in the middle and curl the ends into circles like a pretzel. Carefully place the buns on a greased cookie sheet, cover, and let rise until they are doubled in size.

When ready to bake, preheat oven to 350°F. In a small dish, beat the egg with the water. Using a pastry brush, lightly brush the tops of the buns with the egg wash. Decorate with raisins. Bake for 15 to 20 minutes, or until golden brown.

Gröt
(Rice Pudding)

This dessert is a traditional Swedish favorite.

Serves 6–8

Ingredients
1 teaspoon butter or margarine
1 cup rice
1 cup water
4 cups milk
1/4 cup sugar
1 almond
whipped cream
sugar
cinnamon

Directions
Put the butter or margarine, rice, water, and a pinch of cinnamon in a medium saucepan and bring to a boil. Reduce the heat and simmer until all of the water has been absorbed. Add the milk and sugar, and simmer for another 45 minutes, stirring occasionally. Remove from the heat and stir in the almond. Top with whipped cream and dust with sugar and cinnamon. Traditionally, the one who finds the almond will be the next to marry.

Swedish Meatballs

A traditional Swedish dish, enjoyed all over the world.

Serves 4

Ingredients
Meatballs:
1 egg
1 cup soft bread crumbs
1 teaspoon brown sugar
1/2 teaspoon salt
1/4 teaspoon pepper
1/4 teaspoon ginger
1/4 teaspoon ground cloves
1/4 teaspoon nutmeg
1/4 teaspoon cinnamon
1/2 cup milk
cooking oil

Sour Cream Sauce:
2 tablespoons butter
2 tablespoons flour
1 cup beef broth
1/2 teaspoon salt
dash cayenne pepper
1/2 teaspoon Worcestershire sauce
1 cup dairy sour cream, room temperature

Directions
Mix thoroughly all of the ingredients for the meatballs except the oil. Form into 12 meatballs. Fry in hot oil, about 1-inch deep, until

fully cooked, turning only once. Drain completely on paper towels.

Pour all excess oil from fry pan. Add the
butter to the pan, and stir in the flour. Cook until
bubbly; do not let it brown. Add broth, salt,
cayenne pepper, and Worcestershire sauce;
cook, stirring until thickened (the sauce will not
reach its full thickness until it boils). Empty sour
cream into a large bowl. Add a small amount of
the sauce to the sour cream and stir. Gradually
add in the rest of the sauce, stirring constantly.
Fold meatballs into sauce. Spoon into a chafing
dish, stainless steel, or enamel pan. Heat gently
to serving temperature. Serve with boiled potatoes or hot noodles. Garnish with minced pars-
ley.

Project and Report Ideas

Maps

- Make a map of the eurozone, and create a legend to indicate key manufacturing industries throughout the EU.
- Create an export map of Sweden using a legend to represent all the major products exported by Sweden. The map should clearly indicate all of Sweden's industrial regions.

Reports

- Write a brief report on Sweden's automobile industry.
- The Swedish policy of neutrality during the world wars helped to create dramatic economic growth. Write a report on Sweden's trade during wartime.
- Write a report on Sweden's concerns within the EU.
- Write a brief report on the Swedish welfare system.

Biographies
Write a one-page biography on one of the following:

- Alfred Nobel
- Ingmar Bergman
- Dag Hammarskjöld
- King Carl XVI Gustaf

Journals

- Imagine you are on vacation in Sweden. Write a journal describing your travels. What places do you think are important to visit, and why?
- Read more about industrialist Alfred Nobel. Imagine you are Alfred Nobel. Write a journal about your life and what makes you decide to create the Nobel Prizes.

Projects

- Learn the Swedish expressions for simple words such as hello, good day, please, thank you. Try them on your friends.
- Make a calendar of your country's festivals and list the ones that are common or similar in Sweden. Are they celebrated differently in Sweden? If so, how?
- Go online or to the library and find images of Viking ships. Create a model of one.
- Make a poster showing a Swedish tourist destination you'd like to visit.
- Make a list of all the rivers, places, seas, and islands that you have read about in this book and indicate them on a map of Sweden.
- Find a Swedish recipe other than the ones given in this book, and ask an adult to help you make it. Share it with members of your class.

Group Activity

- Debate: One side should take the role of Germany and the other Sweden. Germany's position is that EU should have greater control over the policies of individual member states, while Sweden will speak in defense of maintaining its own laws and neutrality.

CHRONOLOGY

9000 BCE	Petroglyphs are carved by Sweden's earliest human inhabitants.
98 CE	The Roman historian Tacitus describes a tribe of peoples called the Suiones, now recognized as Swedes.
793	Vikings emerge as the dominant power in Sweden.
1066	King Harald is defeated while invading England, marking the end of the Viking Age.
1397	Sweden joins Denmark under the Kalmar Union.
1523	The Kalmar Union is dissolved.
1658	The Swedish Empire is at the height of its power.
1718	Sweden loses the Great Northern War. Her foreign holdings are seized, and a limited monarchy is established with the creation of the Riksdag.
1772	King Gustav reestablishes absolute monarchy.
1809	A new constitution is adopted.
1815	The Dutch monarchy is established.
1905	Norway officially separates from Sweden.
1914	World War I begins; Sweden remains neutral.
1917	Constitutional monarchy is founded on parliamentary democracy.
1921	Universal suffrage is given to men and women.
1939	World War II begins; Sweden remains neutral.
1946	Sweden joins the United Nations.
1960	Sweden becomes a founding member of EFTA.
1992	EEA agreement is signed.
1993	Sweden begins accession negotiations with the EU.
1995	Sweden joins the EU.

FURTHER READING/INTERNET RESOURCES

Thomas, Keltie. *Sweden, The Land*. New York: Crabtree, 2003.
Thomas, Keltie. *Sweden, The Culture*. New York: Crabtree, 2003.
Thomas, Keltie. *Sweden, The People*. New York: Crabtree, 2003.
Furlong, Kate A., and Kate A. Conley. *Sweden*. Edina, Minn.: ABDO Publishing, 2002.
Yanuck, Debbie L., and Roland Thorstensson. *Many Cultures, One World: Sweden*. Mankato, Minn.:
    Capstone Press, 2004.

Travel Information
www.lonelyplanet.com/destinations/europe/sweden www.travelnotes.org/Europe/sweden.htm

History and Geography
www.luth.se
www.sverigeturism.se/smorgasbord/smorgasbord/society/

Culture and Festivals
www.scandinavica.com
www.sverigeturism.se/smorgasbord/smorgasbord/culture/lifestyle/festivals.html

Economic and Political Information
www.cia.gov/cia/publications/factbook
www.wikipedia.org

EU Information
europa.eu.int

Publisher's note:
The Web sites listed on this page were active at the time of publication. The publisher is not responsible for Web sites that have changed their addresses or discontinued operation since the date of publication. The publisher will review and update the Web-site list upon each reprint.

FOR MORE INFORMATION

Embassy of Sweden
1501 M Street NW
Suite 900
Washington, DC 20005-1702
Tel.: 202-467-2600
Fax: 202-467-2699

Swedish Travel and Tourism Council
Box 3030
Kungsgatan 36
SE-103 61 Stockholm
Sweden
Tel.: 46-8-725-5500
Fax: 46-8-725-5531

Embassy of the United States of America
Dag Hammarskjölds Väg 31
SE-115 89 Stockholm, Sweden
Tel.: 46-8-783-5300

European Union
Delegation of the European Commission to the United States
2300 M Street, NW
Washington, DC 20037
Tel.: 202-862-9500
Fax: 202-429-1766

GLOSSARY

absolute monarchy: A monarchy with complete power and authority.

accession: The formal acceptance by a state of an international treaty or convention.

amalgamation: Something that is a combination of different things.

autonomous: Politically independent and self-governing.

blocs: United groups of countries.

capital: Wealth in the form of property of money.

chancellor: The chief government minister in some parliamentary democracies.

codified: Arranged into an organized system.

coniferous: Characteristic of any tree with thin leaves (needles) that produces cones.

coup d'état: A sudden overthrow of the government and seizure of power.

deciduous: Characteristic of trees and shrubs that shed their leaves in the fall.

dissemination: Widespread distribution of information.

excise: A government-imposed tax on domestic goods.

feudal: Relating to feudalism, a socioeconomic system that existed in medieval Europe in which vassals held land from lords in exchange for military service.

fjords: A long, narrow coastal inlet with steep sides.

Great Depression: A drastic decline in the world economy that resulted in mass unemployment and widespread poverty, which lasted from 1929 to 1939.

landed nobility: Members of the upper class who obtain their status through ownership of land.

maritime: Relating to the sea, ships, or sailing.

mercenaries: Professional soldiers who fight for countries other than their own.

nationalist: Intense feelings of pride in one's country.

neutral: Not taking sides in a conflict.

ratified: Officially approved.

socialism: A political or social system in which the means of production and distribution are controlled by the people and operated according to fairness and equity, not market principles.

solidarity: Standing together as a show of unity.

sovereignty: Ability to rule without outside interference.

stagnancy: A period of inactivity.

suffrage: The right to vote.

tariff: A government-imposed tax on imports.

trade monopolies: Exclusive rights to trade in a particular market or in a particular commodity.

welfare state: A social system in which the state assumes responsibility for the social welfare of its citizens.

Index

PICTURE CREDITS

BIOGRAPHIES

AUTHOR

Heather Docalavich first developed an interest in the history and cultures of Europe through her work as a genealogy researcher. She currently resides in Hilton Head, South Carolina, with her four children.

SERIES CONSULTANTS

Ambassador John Bruton served as Irish Prime Minister from 1994 until 1997. As prime minister, he helped turn Ireland's economy into one of the fastest-growing in the world. He was also involved in the Northern Ireland Peace Process, which led to the 1998 Good Friday Agreement. During his tenure as Ireland's prime minister, he also presided over the European Union presidency in 1996 and helped finalize the Stability and Growth Pact, which governs management of the euro. Before being named the European Commission Head of Delegation in the United States, he was a member of the convention that drafted the European Constitution, signed October 29, 2004.

The European Commission Delegation to the United States represents the interests of the European Union as a whole, much as ambassadors represent their countries' interests to the U.S. government. Matters coming under European Commission authority are negotiated between the commission and the U.S. administration.